SPECTACULAR MARRIAGE

10 SURPRISING WAYS TO DIVORCE PROOF YOUR MARRIAGE

Victoria Mary Fach

BALBOA.PRESS
A DIVISION OF HAY HOUSE

Balboa Press books may be ordered through booksellers or by contacting:

Balboa Press
A Division of Hay House
1663 Liberty Drive
Bloomington, IN 47403
www.balboapress.com
844-682-1282

Because of the dynamic nature of the Internet, any web addresses or links contained in this book may have changed since publication and may no longer be valid. The views expressed in this work are solely those of the author and do not necessarily reflect the views of the publisher, and the publisher hereby disclaims any responsibility for them.

The author of this book does not dispense medical advice or prescribe the use of any technique as a form of treatment for physical, emotional, or medical problems without the advice of a physician, either directly or indirectly. The intent of the author is only to offer information of a general nature to help you in your quest for emotional and spiritual well-being. In the event you use any of the information in this book for yourself, which is your constitutional right, the author and the publisher assume no responsibility for your actions.

Any people depicted in stock imagery provided by Getty Images are models, and such images are being used for illustrative purposes only. Certain stock imagery © Getty Images.

All bible scriptures are taken from World English Bible (WEB), public domain.

Print information available on the last page.

ISBN: 978-1-9822-7267-8 (sc)
ISBN: 978-1-9822-7269-2 (hc)
ISBN: 978-1-9822-7268-5 (e)

Library of Congress Control Number: 2021915869

Balboa Press rev. date: 01/17/2022

For Wes

**who made my life
spectacular**

"'Be who God meant you to be
and you will set the world on fire."
St. Catherine of Siena

CONTENTS

FOREWORD

Everyone comes to know people in their life who have inspired them simply by their own personal witness, who have served as a source of support and encouragement to them as they live their own particular walk in life. This is especially so for those who live their calling in life well; indeed, without such relationships, it would be impossible to persevere in one's vocation. This is who Wes and Vicki Fach have been for me. My friendship with this couple has been for me not only a precious gift from God, but also both a challenge and support to me in living my own vocation as a priest, and now as a bishop, with the same excellence.

I came to know Wes and Vicki well during the years when we were involved with Worldwide Marriage Encounter, presenting weekends and serving in roles of leadership. Even when I had to step down from this involvement due to a call to work in the Roman Curia at the Vatican, our friendship continued to deepen over the years. One of the many things I learned from Marriage Encounter is that all of us in the Church need each other to live our respective vocations well. In particular, priests and married couples support each other in the unique way God has called each of them to live the nuptial mystery of life in Christ. I frequently speak about this, and perhaps some people might find it strange that I feel so affirmed and supported in my Priesthood by a happy and faithful married couple living God's plan for their marriage well. Perhaps they think that I should feel like I'm missing out on something great in life, and so I should feel sad. But I would invite them to reflect: who inspires them to live their own vocation of marriage well – the happy, faithful, zealous priest, or the grumpy, cynical, disillusioned priest?

When I give the example of couples living their vocation of marriage extraordinarily well, and who challenge and affirm me in doing the same in my own vocation, Wes and Vicki Fach always come to mind. They have truly lived St. Mother Theresa of Calcutta's reminder to us that holiness in life consists not in doing extraordinary things, but in doing ordinary things with extraordinary love. Which is why their marriage has been such an extraordinary blessing not only to them, but to all those who have been blessed to know them.

Now Vicki is living her unexpected vocation to widowhood with the same excellence and fidelity, placing her considerable intellectual and spiritual gifts at the service of those open and willing to learn from them. "Spectacular Marriage: Ten Surprising Ways to

Divorce-Proof Your Marriage" is the fruit of her fidelity in accepting the greatest tragedy in her life – the untimely loss of her beloved husband Wes – as a new cross God has given her, a new form of service to Him and to others. This short but substantive book will be an invaluable aid to all couples seeking to live their vocation of marriage for what it is: a sacred calling from God to enter into a school of self-perfection, a path to holiness for themselves and a witness to others to support them in likewise responding to God's call in their own life. Its very brevity, indeed, adds to its usefulness. Husbands and wives are busier now than ever before, but it will not be too difficult for them to make the time to read and discuss how to implement for themselves the wisdom contained in this little treasure chest.

If I may be so bold, though: there is, I believe, an eleventh way for a couple to divorce-proof their marriage that I saw demonstrated in the marital relationship between Wes and Vicki Fach that Vicki does not mention, probably because she is too humble to do so. Being a couple with such depth of wisdom, love, faith and personal experience, they always had much to teach other people. But they never called attention to themselves for this; instead, they were always ready to learn from other couples, especially those with more experience than they, in how to live their marriage well. As good as they were at marriage, they never settled for good enough; extraordinary as they were in their love for each other and their family, they always knew they could, and so they strove, to do better.

It is no secret that very much work needs to be done to rebuild a marriage culture in our society today. It is my hope that this book you hold in your hands right now will be a help for you to do so in your own lives. Strengthening marriages one at a time, giving couples the tools they need to persevere in good times and in bad, for richer and for poorer, in sickness and in health, we can reclaim the beauty and extraordinary grace for everyone that is God's plan for a joy-filled marriage. And I pray that every priest and deacon will read this book, too, and give it as a gift to the couples whose marriages they witness in the name of the Church. Then we will understand that the command not to tear asunder what God has joined, far from a repressive restriction on freedom, is indeed quite the opposite: the sacrament of God's unconditional love for us in His Son Jesus Christ, who is the truth who sets us free.

Thank you, Vicki!
Most Reverend Salvatore J. Cordileone
Archbishop of San Francisco

ACKNOWLEDGEMENTS

This book would not have been written without the love and support of my six children, five sons-in-law, and 24 grandchildren, the wise counsel of my spiritual advisor, Fr. David Exner, the guidance of my friend and business partner, Reni Cordell, and the friendship and editing prowess of Cori Brown.

Deborah Hurwitz of Productivity for Perfectionists has been my inspiration and coach during the writing of the book, and Kate Dorsey is the coach who cheered me on over the final hurdle.

ACKNOWLEDGMENTS

INTRODUCTION

When I started writing this book, originally called *Ten Ways to Divorce-Proof Your Marriage*, if I mentioned it to someone, she or he would say, "Oh, I'd like to have a copy of that book!" In the current atmosphere of no-fault divorce resulting in an unstable landscape for marriage, many couples believe that no marriage is truly secure. Most of us have seen the earthquake of divorce roar through the lives of family and friends, leaving families shattered, where the resulting devastation can never be undone. Our son summed it up succinctly. He was 20 years old when my husband died. He made a good friend in college, whose parents were divorced. When his friend learned that my son's father had died and was expressing his sympathy, my son looked at him and said, "I'd rather he died than that my parents had ever gotten divorced."

Jeff Cavins, who has produced many in-depth Bible studies, points out in a blog episode, **"God's Genius Bar for Marriage,"** that marriage is not a contract but a covenant. A contract can be broken; if someone agrees to sell a book and the other person doesn't give him the money expected, the contract is broken and the seller keeps the book. A covenant such as marriage, however, is an exchange of persons and cannot be broken. Even if one person breaks the covenant, the other one is still bound by it. The first covenant, between God and Abraham, was sealed when Abraham brought a heifer, she-goat, ram, turtledove and young pigeon, *"split them in two, and placed each half opposite the other"* (Genesis 15:10). The blood from the sacrifice ran into the trench between the two sides, and *"a smoking furnace and a flaming torch"* (Genesis 15:17) passed between the pieces. Abraham most likely walked between the split carcasses, indicating that if he should break the covenant it should be done to him as to the sacrificial animals.

Every couple considering marriage should ponder this passage in Genesis to understand the seriousness of what they are undertaking. *Spectacular Marriage* is a guide to working toward a happy marriage in the real world, not a story from a fairy tale where the trials end with the wedding.

I hope this book will distill the essence of what my husband and I learned during 38 adventurous years of marriage and 30 rewarding years of ministry to married couples and their families. The path is challenging; however, marriage is intended to be a glorious vocation that lasts a lifetime, and not just a fairy tale that shimmers away into the mist. It is crucial to invest in it both before and throughout marriage.

Convincing a young couple in love that they need to do something to give their relationship long-term staying power can be an uphill battle. When my husband and I were engaged, I was convinced that we could teach married couples a thing or two, and we probably would have regarded anything other than filling out the necessary forms as a waste of time. It is one of the reasons why the Catholic Church now requires marriage preparation; however, that preparation can often be aimed at the lowest common denominator. One of our daughters and her fiancé found during their preparation for marriage that there was only one area they had not discussed before.

To those just beginning to seek a partner in marriage, I hope this book will help you keep your eyes wide open rather than allow them to be blinded by infatuation. For those who have fallen in love and those who are engaged already, I hope this will provide a vision to evaluate wisely whether to proceed toward marriage and an ever-growing love, or to end a relationship now and save years of heartbreak down the road.

For those who are married, may you find the grace to accept the challenge to enrich your marriage every day, to grow beyond a marriage that is "just fine" to one that is exceptional, with blessings rippling out to your family and friends and beyond.

I have included questions to think about at the end of each chapter. Please feel free to write in this book, answering the questions, underlining or jotting down thoughts you have as you are reading it.

If you are dating, engaged or married, give a copy of the book to the other person or your spouse so that he or she can answer the questions as well. Then exchange your answers and spend some time discussing them. This will open new paths for learning more about one another. With each one, I include the question, "How do I feel about my answer?"

This is a key part of the discussion, because feelings are pathways to intimacy and growth in your relationship. They are spontaneous inner reactions to something that has happened or that you are thinking about. We are more likely to share our thoughts than our feelings. Our thoughts tend to be more on the surface whereas when we share our feelings, we are revealing deeper, more vulnerable parts of ourselves. Sharing our feelings and listening to another's feelings with our hearts is the passageway to tenderizing our relationships, particularly in marriage.

When my husband and I were part of a presenting team on a Worldwide Marriage Encounter Weekend, we spent a good part of one of the early talks explaining the difference between thoughts and feelings. Thoughts come from the head and feelings from the heart. There is a very easy way to distinguish them, and once you are aware of this, you will discover how often people describe them inaccurately. If you can say "I feel _____" you're sharing a feeling. If you say "I feel that _____" it's a thought.

You can feel sad, happy, angry, tired, and many other emotions. But if you say, "I feel that you should do the dishes/put the kids to bed/get up earlier in the morning/be nicer to my mother," you are expressing a thought. To be accurate you should say, "I believe that" or "I think that" whatever the phrase was that came after "that."

You can argue with thoughts, but feelings are just inner reactions that have no morality. They just are. They are also windows into the soul, letting us see the inner life of the person who is sharing them. If that person is our husband or wife, we can journey together into our hearts and souls, not just our minds, letting us see the inner life of the person who is sharing them. If that person is our husband or wife, we can reach levels of intimacy that can be attained in no other way.

My beloved husband and I wrote each other a love letter every day for the last 30 years of our marriage. We described our feelings in detail and then chose one feeling to try to understand more fully. For instance, if I was describing a feeling of exhaustion, I might say, "I feel exhausted as if I had run a marathon. I feel worn out, as if I had been chasing the children around all day and had gotten nothing else done. I feel utterly flattened, as if a bulldozer had just rolled over me." We would then discuss the feeling until my husband understood what I had been sharing. We either took turns focusing on one of our feelings, or if one feeling were stronger, we'd talk about that. Over the years, we developed an ever-deepening bond, and our relationship grew more intimate as we fell more deeply in love. Getting to know another person in such a way is an adventure because every person has infinite depths. In the 38 years we were married, we were constantly discovering new facets of our love. Although I have lost him in this world, I know that I was deeply loved and that in our time together, we left nothing unsaid.

QUESTIONS TO PONDER

If I am single, am I willing to take the time to discover if I am called to be married? How do I feel about my answer?

_____

_____

_____

_____

_____

_____

_____

_____

_____

_____

_____

_____

_____

_____

_____

_____

_____

_____

_____

Am I willing to think seriously about what I am searching for in a marriage partner? How do I feel about my answer?

_____

_____

_____

_____

_____

_____

_____

_____

_____

_____

_____

_____

_____

_____

_____

_____

_____

_____

If I am engaged, am I willing to use the tools available to me to determine whether or not I should continue in my engagement? How do I feel about my answer?

_____

_____

_____

_____

_____

_____

_____

_____

_____

_____

_____

_____

_____

_____

_____

_____

_____

_____

_____

_____

If I am married, am I willing to invest in every resource we can find to make our marriage spectacular? How do I feel about my answer?

_____

_____

_____

_____

_____

_____

_____

_____

_____

_____

_____

_____

_____

_____

_____

_____

_____

_____

CHAPTER 1
Share the Faith

The foundational path for a strong marriage is to marry someone who shares the same faith as you do. I have spoken with many who struggle in their marriages because the spouse has a different faith or none at all.

In the glow of romantic love, we can think that it doesn't matter and love will conquer all. If faith is important to us, those differences will loom more significant as the marriage matures and particularly when children arrive. It is difficult to convince a child that your faith is the key to salvation when your spouse believes and behaves differently.

I was raised in a Catholic home, and my mother particularly emphasized the importance of finding a

Catholic husband. She had been engaged to a good Baptist man, who looked into the Catholic faith, but he just couldn't believe in her religion. My mother broke her engagement to him when she met my father, who was Catholic. After he died, I discovered that he had had many questions about the Catholic faith after he came home from serving in the Pacific in World War II. He wrote to the Knights of Columbus for one of their correspondence courses in the Catholic faith. When the Knights discovered that he was about to complete his PhD in physics, they asked the rector of the seminary to be in charge of the correspondence. The rector was not only up to my father's intellectual weight, but he had a wonderful sense of humor, as did my father. Reading my father's journey to an adult faith through those letters gave me an even greater appreciation of all that he passed on to me.

When I began dating Wes, my mother frequently pointed out that he wasn't Catholic, and I responded that I was just dating him, not marrying him. Of course, she was right when she said that dating someone often leads to marriage. By the time I was in college, Wes and I were becoming more serious about our relationship, but I also knew that I didn't want to marry someone who wasn't Catholic. I wrote a prayer asking God to grant Wes the gift of the Catholic faith, and I prayed it every day.

When I was a child, I went to a Catholic school and was blessed with wonderful Ursuline nuns who inspired me to think about a vocation to the religious life. As I thought about my relationship with Wes and pondered the future, I wondered if God was still calling me to become a nun. I was praying outside our home at night the summer before my sophomore year of college. The Texas sky was filled with brilliant stars, and I felt suspended between earth and heaven. I reached the point where I was able to tell God that if he wanted me to marry Wes, he would have to convert him. If he didn't, I would take that as an indication that I should pursue a religious vocation. As I prayed, a wave of peace engulfed me, and I was perfectly open to God's will for me.

That Thanksgiving, I flew back to New Jersey from Texas. I hesitantly asked Wes, "Have you ever, um, maybe thought about, uh, looking into the Catholic Church?"

He replied that he had been taking instructions and would be received into the Church on Palm Sunday. I was dumbstruck with joy. I had no idea he had even thought about it, and God had answered my prayer dramatically! Wes later told me that when he had decided to become Catholic (after basically reading his way into the Church), he thought in a vague way that I would be pleased. He'd had no idea then that it was so critical to our relationship from my point of view. I wanted him to become Catholic because he believed in the truths of the faith, not because I would like it. By then, I knew that he would never become Catholic unless he could assent intellectually to the faith. He told me later that a friend of his who was leaving the Church as he was preparing to enter, asked him why he was doing it, and Wes replied simply, "Because I came to believe that it was true."

After we married, he became the leader of the faith in our home, and we had many lively discussions about aspects of the faith throughout our married years and worked together to pass it on to our children. He was curious about what it was like to grow up in the Church before Vatican II and would often ask me questions about what the Mass was like when it was a Double, Second Class. (There was a very complex hierarchy of feasts in the Church including Double of the I Class, Double of the II Class, Greater Double or Major Double and Double, in order of descending rank, which was eliminated after Vatican II.) I had no idea; I remembered seeing things like that written in my missal but hadn't the faintest idea what they meant. My husband was truly delighted when the priest who baptized our son was made a bishop and they could discuss all the tiniest details of the Tridentine Mass when celebrated by a bishop. As a lawyer, my husband was fascinated by canon law, and was one of the few laypeople who could discuss canon law in detail with our bishop, who had served on the Apostolic Signatura, the highest judicial authority in the Catholic Church apart from the pope.

I close this chapter with a poem I wrote about that moment of decision when I surrendered to God's will for my future.

4

PYROTECHNICS

Also in a garden--in Austin—
Spirit's rich silence bolts creation to sound
(crickets loud as gunshots at Town Lake
on New Year's Eve), night noise
evokes colors from the Texas wind
to flames that whisper the world asunder
with thundering stillness.
A solidity of peace enkindles
the shining clarion of a French horn
against a flat dark portrait of strings,
an alabaster song of yes and yes and yes.
The gathering rush of dawn is fused
into a long-held twilight pause.
The great starry doors of the indigo sky swing wide--
immersed in light, the soul ignites:
tinderbox of joy.

QUESTIONS TO PONDER

How important is my faith to me? How do I feel about my answer?

_____

_____

_____

_____

_____

_____

_____

_____

_____

_____

_____

_____

_____

_____

_____

_____

_____

_____

_____

How important is it to me that my (future) spouse share the same faith? How do I feel about my answer?

_____

_____

_____

_____

_____

_____

_____

_____

_____

_____

_____

_____

_____

_____

_____

_____

_____

_____

_____

_____

Do I talk about my faith with the person I am dating or am engaged to, or with my spouse? How do I feel about my answer?

_____

_____

_____

_____

_____

_____

_____

_____

_____

_____

_____

_____

_____

_____

_____

_____

_____

CHAPTER 2
Happily Ever After

The second way to pursue a divorce-proof marriage is to marry someone committed to marriage for life. Because my husband and I were married in the Catholic Church at a time when marriages were expected to last, and people were scandalized when they didn't, we took our vows seriously and intended to be married until death separated us.

The Church makes this clear as the priest introduces the declaration of intentions:

"My dear friends, you have come together in this church so that the Lord may seal and strengthen your love in the presence of the Church's minister and this community. Christ abundantly blesses this love. He has already consecrated you in baptism and now he enriches and strengthens you by a special sacrament so that you may assume the duties of marriage in mutual and lasting fidelity."

The Catholic Church sees Christ's first miracle at a wedding feast as a confirmation of the goodness of marriage and "the proclamation that thenceforth marriage will be an efficacious sign of Christ's presence" (Catechism of the Catholic Church #1613), or what the Church defines as a sacrament. The nuptial covenant between God and his people Israel is reflected in the image of exclusive and faithful married love. The Sacrament of Matrimony enters a new dimension and reveals "the new and everlasting covenant in which the Son of God, by becoming incarnate and giving his life, has united to himself in a certain way all mankind saved by him" (CCC #1612), a covenant celebrated in Revelation as "the wedding supper of the Lamb" (Revelation 19:9).

The apostle Paul emphasizes this in his often misunderstood hymn on matrimony. "Husbands, love your wives, even as Christ also loved the assembly and gave himself up for her" (Eph. 5:25). Before women walk out of church when they hear "Wives, be subject to your own husbands, as to the Lord" (Ephesians 5:22), which comes right after the command that husbands and wives should be "subjecting yourselves to one another in the fear of Christ" (Ephesians 5:21), we should consider that the wife is only being asked to be subordinate, but the husband is being asked to give up his life for his wife! Then Paul provides a sublime parallel: "a man will leave his father and mother and will be joined to his wife. Then the two will become one flesh. This mystery is great, but I speak concerning Christ and the assembly" (Ephesians 5:31-32).

After we had been married for quite a few years, one of my husband's coworkers asked him if, being a lawyer, he had drawn up a pre-nuptial contract for us. He replied that the contract he used was "to have and to hold from this day forward; for better, for worse, for richer, for poorer, in sickness and in health, to love and to cherish, till death us do part."

These days, when a much higher percentage of marriages end in divorce, and cohabitation is more socially accepted, it is critical to be certain that the person being considered for marriage believes that marriage is permanent. A potential spouse should show that he or she honors other commitments undertaken. People who frequently break promises or back out of things they said they'd do are not good marriage material. Warning flags should go up over someone who is divorced; failing at one marriage is an indicator that a lifetime commitment to marriage has not been a value.

If someone is civilly divorced, but the marriage has been annulled by the Catholic Church, this means that the marriage never took place, and he or she is free to marry. However, it is perhaps even more important to take the time to get to know one another if contemplating a marriage with someone whose marriage has been annulled to be certain that the proper outlook on marriage exists, and that the necessary healing from the earlier relationship has taken place.

In addition, think critically about the things that are most important in marriage besides faith and commitment. Neil Clark Warren's book, ***How to Know if Someone Is Worth Pursuing in Two Dates or Less***[1] is invaluable in helping individuals discover the qualities that are essential and those that are deal-breakers in a future spouse. Warren writes, "You need to rehearse the fact that a bad marriage is a thousand times worse than no marriage at all." Those who have seen friends in a catastrophic marriage or one that ends in divorce can testify to the truth of that statement, and the devastating effects of divorce. Carefully evaluating a potential marriage partner is an essential investment in building a future with the right person. Critical qualities and those that don't matter vary from one person to another, so it is important to understand oneself and the things important to each.

---

[1] Neil Clark Warren, *How to Know if Someone is Worth Pursuing in Two Dates or Less* (Nashville: Thomas Nelson Publishers, 1999)

QUESTIONS TO PONDER

What are the most important values for me in marriage?
How do I feel about that?

_____

_____

_____

_____

_____

_____

_____

_____

_____

_____

_____

_____

_____

_____

_____

_____

_____

_____

_____

Have I discussed these values with the person I am dating/ engaged to/ my spouse? How do I feel about my answer?

_____

_____

_____

_____

_____

_____

_____

_____

_____

_____

_____

_____

_____

_____

_____

_____

_____

_____

If our values are significantly different, should I continue in a dating relationship or in an engagement? How do I feel about my answer?

_____

_____

_____

_____

_____

_____

_____

_____

_____

_____

_____

_____

_____

_____

_____

_____

_____

_____

_____

If I am married, how can I work to overcome our differences? How do I feel about my answer?

_____

_____

_____

_____

_____

_____

_____

_____

_____

_____

_____

_____

_____

_____

_____

_____

_____

_____

_____

CHAPTER 3
Wedding Vows

If the first two ways to divorce-proof your marriage focus on marrying the right person, the third is part of the more immediate preparation. Avoid the temptation to write creative wedding vows. In many churches, including the Catholic Church, the vows are part of the official liturgy and generally can't be changed. In some churches or where the bride and groom are getting married in a civil ceremony, there is a lot of leeway for the vows to have a tendency to trivialize the seriousness of what is being undertaken, and often water down the lifetime commitment the vows should express. Some of them go on and on at great length and say basically what traditional vows cover with rococo additions and, sadly, even ungrammatical constructions, as in "I will look with joy down the path of our tomorrow's" (sic). Use other avenues to express your creativity—the dress, the cake, and the reception. More importantly, astonish others with building an extraordinary and enduring marriage. Vows are not just a lyric paean to the beauty of your love, but a statement of the covenant of marriage being undertaken that reflects a legal and spiritual bond.

The Episcopal Wedding Ceremony taken from *The Book of Common Prayer* [2] is a beautiful summation of what God intends for married couples.

Then the Celebrant, facing the people and the persons to be married, with the woman to the right and the man to the left, addresses the congregation and says

Dearly beloved: We have come together in the presence of God to witness and bless the joining together of this man and this woman in Holy Matrimony. The bond and covenant of marriage was established by God in creation, and our Lord Jesus Christ adorned this manner of life by his presence and first miracle at a wedding in Cana of Galilee. It signifies to us the mystery of the union between Christ and his Church, and Holy Scripture commends it to be honored among all people.

The union of husband and wife in heart, body, and

---

[2] The Episcopal Church (1979), *The Book of Common Prayer* (1979), Oxford University Press

mind is intended by God for their mutual joy; for the help and comfort given one another in prosperity and adversity; and, when it is God's will, for the procreation of children and their nurture in the knowledge and love of the Lord. Therefore marriage is not to be entered into unadvisedly or lightly, but reverently, deliberately, and in accordance with the purposes for which it was instituted by God.

Into this holy union N.N. and N.N. now come to be joined.

If any of you can show just cause why they may not lawfully be married, speak now; or else for ever hold your peace.

Then the Celebrant says to the persons to be married I require and charge you both, here in the presence of God, that if either of you know any reason why you may not be united in marriage lawfully, and in accordance with God's Word, you do now confess it. The Declaration of Consent The Celebrant says to the woman

N., will you have this man to be your husband; to live together in the covenant of marriage? Will you love him, comfort him, honor and keep him, in sickness and in health; and, forsaking all others, be faithful to him as long as you both shall live?

The Woman answers

I will.

The Celebrant says to the man

N., will you have this woman to be your wife; to live together in the covenant of marriage? Will you love her, comfort her, honor and keep her, in sickness and in health; and, forsaking all others, be faithful to her as long as you both shall live?

The Man answers

I will.

Thus entering into the covenant of marriage, the couple declares their intention to be faithful to their vows to each other as long as they both shall live, a steadfast promise that will give them security throughout their lives together.

QUESTIONS TO PONDER

If I am preparing for marriage, have I learned what the vows are that are specific to my faith tradition? How do I feel about that?

_____

_____

_____

_____

_____

_____

_____

_____

_____

_____

_____

_____

_____

_____

_____

_____

_____

_____

_____

VICTORIA MARY FACH

If I am married, can I look back at the vows we exchanged and see how I am living up to them? How do I feel about that?

_____

_____

_____

Do I see wedding vows as expressing a contract or a covenant? How do I feel about that?

_____

_____

_____

_____

_____

_____

_____

_____

_____

_____

_____

_____

_____

_____

_____

_____

_____

_____

_____

CHAPTER 4
Ready, Set...

For an engaged couple, an important step toward divorce-proofing the upcoming marriage is to attend an Engaged Encounter (EE) Weekend or Evenings for the Engaged, if they are available. The EE Weekend helps a couple look at every area of their future life together, from religious faith to jobs, money, sex, children, family, and other aspects of married life. Often, couples have never talked about many of these areas. There may be several answers to these questions where one or the other is surprised at what their future husband or wife thinks.

The Engaged Encounter Weekend includes a series of presentations led by a team of married couples and a priest, who encourage each couple to talk privately about their upcoming marriage from the point of view of their own relationship. Personal reflection and couple discussion help reveal attitudes that can impact the marriage. The motto of Engaged Encounter, "A wedding is a day, a marriage is a lifetime," highlights the importance of serious preparation for a lifetime as a married couple who will positively affect their own family and the world around them.

A friend of ours who gave EE Weekends, told us that the teams often judged it a successful Weekend if at least one of the couples making the Weekend broke off their engagement after discovering incompatibility on serious issues. It is far better to discover this during the engagement than after marriage.

This is much better immediate preparation than my husband and I experienced. We met with my pastor and filled out some forms (which were in Latin) and possibly discussed marriage, but it left very little impression on me if we did. I'm sure we chose the Readings for the Nuptial Mass, although the priest who married us asked if we could change the Gospel Reading to Matthew 7:24-27, about the two foundations. I still remember how in his homily he emphasized that our marriage would be built solidly on the rock of the Church, and so it was.

We also had had 5 years getting to know each other, from the time I was 17 and Wes was 16 until we were married at 22. This time included 3 years of writing love letters to each other while we were away at college, half a country apart, when we discussed all that we were thinking and experiencing as we were becoming adults. I was thinking seriously about marriage all through college and wrote a paper on marriage as it was portrayed in Dostoevsky's four major novels when I was taking Russian Literature. In addition, we paid attention to things we didn't want in our marriage as we saw people whom we knew going through separation and divorce. We also had the good example of many other couples in happy relationships, who were married over 50 years.

We were an unusual couple in terms of how much we had studied about the Sacrament of Matrimony, but I'm sure we would have benefited from an Engaged Encounter Weekend if they had existed then. These Weekends take couples in good engaged relationships and bring them to the next level, even when couples are convinced that no one could be more deeply in love than they are! They also point out that the couple is not getting married in a vacuum, but in a community and world that needs the witness of their faithful and passionate married love.

QUESTIONS TO PONDER

If I am dating or engaged, how much time and energy am I focusing on getting to know the other person's values, dreams for his or her life, and beliefs about marriage? How do I feel about my answer?

_____

_____

_____

_____

_____

_____

_____

_____

_____

_____

_____

_____

_____

_____

_____

_____

_____

Do we talk about serious issues like our religious faith, jobs, money, sex, children, and how to live out the vocation of marriage? How do I feel about my answer?

_____

_____

_____

_____

_____

_____

_____

_____

_____

_____

_____

_____

_____

_____

_____

_____

_____

_____

CHAPTER 5
Increasing the Odds

The lure of living together is a passionate and ultimately rocky path that can interfere with dreams of a strong and lasting marriage. Couples have been misled into thinking that they can "try out" marriage by acting as if they are married to see if they are compatible; however, there is an essential difference between cohabitation with no commitment and a covenant where a man and a woman become one flesh and promise to love each other until death ends their relationship.

Statistics collected by the US Attorney Legal Service show that a couple who cohabits risks a 49 percent chance of divorce within 5 years rather than a 20 percent chance of being divorced if they do not live together before marriage. If a couple believes they can sidestep the issue by living together *instead of* marrying, 49 percent of them are likely to break up within 5 years. The percentage who break up within 10 years is 62 percent, again nearly double the 33 percent for a married couple. Only half of cohabiting couples marry within 5 years. Living together can often be more stressful due to instability exacerbated by lack of a permanent commitment.

Society doesn't often condemn a couple for living together; however, couples who come from a religious background or who stop to think about what they are doing will frequently have the uneasy sense that they are "living in sin," even if they are not willing to admit it. In *Brideshead Revisited* Julia realized that she was "living in sin, with sin, by sin, for sin, every hour, every day, year in, year out. Waking up with sin in the morning, seeing the curtains drawn on sin, bathing it, showing it round, giving it a good time, putting it to sleep at night...." [3]

Waiting to live together until marriage not only increases chances of a long and happy marriage but avoids having to live with the constant companion of guilt.

---

[3] Evelyn Waugh, *Brideshead Revisited* (New York, Boston, London: Little, Brown and Company, 1944)

QUESTIONS TO PONDER

Did I know the statistics on living together before marriage and the probability of having a lasting marriage? How do I feel about that?

_____

_____

_____

_____

_____

_____

_____

_____

_____

_____

_____

_____

_____

_____

_____

_____

_____

_____

What are the advantages of waiting until marriage for sexual intimacy? How do I feel about that?

_____

_____

_____

_____

_____

_____

_____

_____

_____

_____

_____

_____

_____

_____

_____

_____

_____

_____

CHAPTER 6
Learn Deep Communication

Choosing the path of sexual purity opens the gate to a spectacular trail where you can enter deeply into coming to know the other person emotionally and spiritually. Couples should learn each other's likes and dislikes, their dreams for the future and interests in the present. The marriage preparation programs Engaged Encounter and Evenings for the Engaged plunge a couple into communication about the areas that matter the most after marriage and offer tools that can deepen communication throughout married life. By choosing not to live together in a sham of marriage, a couple can then focus on getting to know each other in ways other than physical, which can short-circuit deep communication before marriage. Spiritual, emotional and mental intimacy will provide a firm foundation on which to build the physical intimacy designed to begin on the wedding day.

Each human being is unique and inexhaustible, and getting to know each other can be an exciting adventure, comparing differences and similarities in thoughts and feelings, backgrounds, families and friends. Even for those who have met while fairly young, there are always things to discover about each other, some trivial, others far more substantial. Similarities can draw a couple together. In discovering differences, decide whether those differences will make living together difficult or perhaps even impossible.

Learn to appreciate differences during the dating period—if they are not deal-breakers for the relationship— so those differences may be valued during marriage. My beloved husband and I discovered when we took a standard personality test that we were the opposite in every category; by then we had been married many years. These differences often made our marriage challenging, but through our work in Worldwide Marriage Encounter, we learned to appreciate our differences.

When we were given the responsibility of coordinating a huge convention, we learned to combine our different strengths to bring about a very successful event. Wes was very organized and was able to plan and time the many different aspects of the convention. I am a people person, and I speak Spanish, and was able to communicate with the Spanish speaking couples involved with the convention. I also translated the final key talk into Spanish.

Wes would usually write the preliminary email drafts to inform our committee of current events and upcoming meetings. I would make it more personal by telling everyone how much we looked forward to being with them.

At one point, Wes was very busy at work and told me to write the initial email and then he'd look at it. I went on and on about how much we loved our committee and were looking forward to the next gathering. He read it and told me it was very good, but that I had forgotten to put the date and time of the meeting in the email! I valued the way he coordinated everything so it all came together at the right time and I felt treasured for my people skills which had often seemed less important in the past. We truly learned what it meant to be a team, both as a couple, and with all the different personalities working with us on the convention.

Take the time to get to know each other. Wes and I met as seniors in high school. I treasure the memories of all those years through college and his first year two years of law school that we were continually discovering new aspects of our personalities, both through correspondence in college (when we were half a country apart), and the last year when we saw each other every day since we lived two subway stops apart in New York City.

Discovering irreconcilable differences makes it much easier to break off the relationship when dating, or even to cancel wedding plans when engaged. Wes and I told our daughters they could tell us they had changed their minds a minute before the wedding began, and we meant it. Investing the time and effort to get to know the person you are dating or to whom you are engaged increases the certainty of building a strong marriage and provides more of the tools to continue learning about each other throughout married life.

QUESTIONS TO PONDER

Am I committed to continually learning more about the person whom I am dating, or to whom I am engaged or married? How do I feel about that?

_____

_____

_____

_____

_____

_____

_____

_____

_____

_____

_____

_____

_____

_____

_____

_____

_____

_____

How alike am I to the person I am dating/engaged to/ married to? How do I feel about that?

_____

_____

_____

_____

_____

_____

_____

_____

_____

_____

_____

_____

_____

_____

_____

_____

_____

_____

_____

If I am dating or engaged to someone who is very different from me, am I willing to consider breaking up rather than settling for the idea of "he'll/she'll do?" How do I feel about that?

_____

_____

_____

_____

_____

_____

_____

_____

_____

_____

_____

_____

_____

_____

_____

_____

_____

_____

_____

Do I see learning more about my spouse as a lifetime adventure? How do I feel about my answer?

_____

_____

_____

_____

_____

_____

_____

_____

_____

_____

_____

_____

_____

_____

_____

_____

_____

CHAPTER 7
Put on the Armor of God

*Put on the whole armor of God, that you may be
able to stand against the wiles of the devil.*

--Ephesians 6:11

When taking up the challenge of married life, be dressed
for the expedition! St. Paul reminds us in the letter to
the Ephesians to put on the armor of God. The best
way to prepare for the challenges that will inevitably
come is to pray with each other and for each other every
day and throughout each day. Marriages have eternal
dimensions that have effects on friends and neighbors
as well as children and succeeding generations. This is

not just a fight against a culture that devalues a lifetime commitment between husband and wife:

> *For our wrestling is not against flesh and blood, but against the principalities, against the powers, against the world's rulers of the darkness of this age, and against the spiritual forces of wickedness in the heavenly places.* [13] *Therefore put on the whole armor of God, that you may be able to withstand in the evil day, and having done all, to stand.* [14] *Stand therefore, having the utility belt of truth buckled around your waist, and having put on the breastplate of righteousness,* [15] *and having fitted your feet with the preparation of the Good News of peace,* [16] *above all, taking up the shield of faith, with which you will be able to quench all the fiery darts of the evil one.* [17] *And take the helmet of salvation, and the sword of the Spirit, which is the word of God.*
>
> —Ephesians 6:12-17

Before we were engaged, I wrote a prayer I said every day that my future fiancé would convert to the Catholic faith. I also began to say the Rosary daily to surround him with the love of the mother of the Redeemer. I prayed for him every day throughout our married life. As he was dying, he told me never to forget to pray for him once he died, and I honor that request. I am convinced that many of the blessings bestowed on our marriage flowed from the prayers we raised up together for each other, our children, and grandchildren.

QUESTIONS TO PONDER

Do I pray for the person I am dating or to whom I'm engaged or married? How do I feel about my answer?

_____

_____

_____

_____

_____

_____

_____

_____

_____

_____

_____

_____

_____

_____

_____

_____

_____

_____

_____

_____

Do I pray **with** the person I am dating or to whom I am engaged or married? How do I feel about my answer?

_____

_____

_____

_____

_____

_____

_____

_____

_____

_____

_____

_____

_____

_____

_____

_____

_____

_____

_____

_____

_____

Do I think it is important to put on the armor of God? How do I feel about my answer?

_____

_____

_____

_____

_____

_____

_____

_____

_____

_____

_____

_____

_____

_____

_____

_____

_____

_____

CHAPTER 8
The Languages of Love

Learning and using one another's love language can greatly enrich and strengthen marriage. My husband and I were introduced to this concept through Gary Chapman's invaluable book, *The Five Love Languages*[4], which identifies five primary ways to express and receive love. The book maintains that each of us tends to experience love primarily through one or two of these languages. When husband and wife have different primary love languages (which is often the case), the trouble begins. When my husband and I were giving weekends based

---

[4] Gary Chapman, *The Five Love Languages* (Chicago: Northfield Publishing, 1992)

on this book, there were usually only one or two couples who had the same love language.

The languages Chapman identifies are:

1. Words of Affirmation
2. Quality Time
3. Receiving Gifts
4. Acts of Service
5. Physical Touch

The book includes an assessment to help husband and wife learn their primary love language, which they can then share with each other. The five love languages include ways to "speak" them so that your partner's "love tank" can stay filled.

There are various "dialects" of these love languages. My husband's primary love language was quality time. Mine was receiving gifts, but my secondary language was also quality time. His love tank could be filled when he was away on a business trip because we talked on the phone every day he was gone, and those conversations were quality time to him. Talking on the phone to him did not fill my love tank at all because he wasn't physically there. If we were both at home, and I was working upstairs in my studio, where I could hear him downstairs talking on the phone, my love tank was being filled. Just knowing he was there nearby helped to fill my love tank.

It's a natural tendency to express our love to our spouse in the language we speak, except in the rare cases where husband and wife have the same love language. It's important to learn to speak the other's love language so love can be given and received. These concepts were presented in weekend retreats with several other couples. It was a beautiful experience to see spouses break through the "silence" that impacted their relationships before they understood the importance of their love languages.

Anyone contemplating marriage would do well to read this book. Share it with the person you're dating or to whom you are engaged. If you are married, do the same with your husband or wife. Then take the time to discuss what you learned and how to apply it in your relationship. It's eye-opening to bring these concepts to disagreements or misunderstandings and will go a long way towards increasing intimacy and deepening love for one another.

QUESTIONS TO PONDER

Am I willing to learn our love languages? How do I feel about my answer?

_____

_____

_____

_____

_____

_____

_____

_____

_____

_____

_____

_____

_____

_____

_____

_____

Do I think that knowing our love languages can help us to fill one another's "love tank?" How do I feel about my answer?

_____

_____

_____

_____

_____

_____

_____

_____

_____

_____

_____

_____

_____

_____

_____

_____

_____

_____

_____

What are some ways that I can fill the love tank of the person I am dating or to whom I am engaged or married? How do I feel about my answer?

_____

_____

_____

_____

_____

_____

_____

_____

_____

_____

_____

_____

_____

_____

_____

_____

_____

_____

CHAPTER 9
Drought-Proofing Marriage

Blessed is the man who trusts in Yahweh,
and whose confidence is in Yahweh.
⁸ For he will be as a tree planted by the waters,
who spreads out its roots by the river,
and will not fear when heat comes,
but its leaf will be green,
and will not be concerned in the year of drought.
It won't cease from yielding fruit.

Jeremiah 17:7-8

He will be like a tree
planted by the streams of water,
That produces its fruit in its season,
whose leaf also does not wither.

Psalm 1:3

"Drought-proofing" marriage is a wise investment to ensure a couple endures for the long haul. Marriage can go through dry spells when the fresh sap of love isn't flowing freely.

Conflict flares up more easily than romance, communication dwindles down to working out schedules and putting out fires, and the flames of passion have been banked down to a few embers in a darkening hearth. Trust in the Lord enables you to sink your roots deeply in his life-giving graces to keep love green and fruitful

One of the best ways to experience love constantly growing and communication that becomes more meaningful is to attend a Worldwide Marriage Encounter Weekend 2 to 5 years after marrying, although it is also wonderful for couples who have been married much longer. The Weekend takes a good marriage and elevates it to extraordinary through communication techniques that enable husbands and wives to reach a depth of understanding that could never have been achieved without the Weekend.

Our intimacy and passion increased throughout the 38 years Wes and I were married because of our Worldwide

Marriage Encounter Weekend. When my beloved husband died, the biggest regret I had was that he had died too soon, but we had left nothing unsaid. Every day we took at least 20 minutes to share our thoughts and feelings with each other. This gave us a depth of understanding and love that we could never have reached without that investment in our relationship. We poured out our love on each other every day, and he left me with a strength that surprised me and the assurance that I had been deeply and truly loved.

QUESTIONS TO PONDER

Do I want to deepen and strengthen my relationship with
my husband or wife? How do I feel about my answer?

_____

_____

_____

_____

_____

_____

_____

_____

_____

_____

_____

_____

_____

_____

Am I willing to give my husband or wife the gift of my time and myself on a Worldwide Marriage Encounter Weekend? How do I feel about my answer?

_____

_____

_____

_____

_____

_____

_____

_____

_____

_____

_____

_____

_____

_____

_____

_____

_____

_____

_____

CHAPTER 10

The Special Secret Sauce

The tenth key to divorce-proofing marriage can be compared to a "special sauce" that enhances the marriage, becomes an intimate part of it and brings it to perfection the way God intended.

> *God created man in his own image.*
> *In God's image he created him;*
> *male and female he created them.*
> *God blessed them. God said to them,*
> *"Be fruitful, multiply, fill the earth, and*
> *subdue it.*

Genesis 1:27-28

In 1979, Pope John Paul II began his extensive series

of Wednesday audiences which were ultimately melded into Theology of the Body and became one of the richest contributions to the theology of marriage. Fr. Chuck Gallagher, the founder of Worldwide Marriage Encounter, brought many of these insights into the Weekend.

We live in a conflicted world, where contraception is seen as the norm, but organic food, fabrics and other items are highly valued. The list of possible side effects of contraceptives printed by the companies (who are getting rich producing and marketing them) is daunting. There is a narrow and somewhat overgrown path for those who would like to space their children or postpone pregnancy for a serious reason. Natural Family Planning (which is NOT the much derided "rhythm method") is truly organic and includes many different approaches from the low-tech which was taught by St. Teresa of Calcutta to illiterate couples to high-tech ovulation monitors that predict days when a woman is fertile. Some of the studies indicate a divorce rate of only about 3% for couples who use Natural Family Planning. (See Lifeissues.net to find the article on "The Practice of Natural Family Planning Versus the Use of Artificial Birth Control.")

Natural Family Planning (NFP) is a method of approaching fertility requiring the cooperation of both husband and wife. It encourages their communication and strengthens their love for one another as a self-giving act of the will, not a "feeling" which can change from day to day. This approach helps the husband and wife see that they are responsible to choose to love their spouse and are not at the mercy of feelings. NFP is more conducive to a lifetime commitment to the marriage, and this provides security and stability both to the couple and to the children who are the fruit of their marriage.

Recently, I saw a poster with a picture of Pope Paul VI, and the headline: "I told you so." When one rereads *Humanae Vitae* in the light of current events, it is clear how prophetic his words were, although furiously criticized ever since the time of its publication.

He delineates some of the serious consequences that result from the use of artificial contraception, which women particularly should note. "Upright men can even better convince themselves of the solid grounds on which the teaching of the Church in this field is based, if they care to reflect upon the consequences of methods of artificial birth control. Let them consider, first of all, how wide and easy a road would thus be opened up towards conjugal infidelity and the general lowering of morality. Not much experience is needed in order to know human weakness, and to understand that men—especially the young, who are so vulnerable on this point—have need of encouragement to be faithful to the moral law, so that they must not be offered some easy means of eluding its observance. It is also to be feared that the man, growing used to the employment of anticonceptive practices, may finally lose respect for the woman and, no longer caring for her physical and psychological equilibrium, may come to the point of considering her as a mere instrument of selfish enjoyment, and no longer as his respected and beloved companion.

"Let it be considered also that a dangerous weapon would thus be placed in the hands of those public authorities who take no heed of moral exigencies. Who could blame a government for applying to the solution of the problems of the community those means acknowledged to be licit for married couples in the solution of a family problem? Who will stop rulers from favoring, from even imposing upon their peoples, if they were to consider it necessary, the method of contraception which they judge to be most efficacious? In such a way men, wishing to avoid individual, family, or social difficulties encountered in the observance of the divine law, would reach the point of placing at the mercy of the intervention of public authorities the most personal and most reserved sector of conjugal intimacy." We only need to consider the "Me Too" movement and the forced sterilizations and abortions in India and China to see how massive the consequences have been.

In contrast to a cascade of serious repercussions that follow the use of artificial contraception, Paul VI presents a beautiful portrait of marriage where the couple is following the laws of God. "This love is first of all fully human, that is to say, of the senses and of the spirit at the same time. It is not, then, a simple transport of instinct and sentiment, but also, and principally, an act of the free will, intended to endure and to grow by means of the joys and sorrows of daily life, in such a way that husband and wife become one only heart and one only soul, and together attain their human perfection."

With artificial contraception, this oneness is undercut. Husband and wife should be saying to each other, "I accept and love you completely," but with artificial contraception, they are saying that they do not accept the gift of their fertility, which goes right to the heart and soul of their relationship. Natural Family Planning is about 98% effective, and a husband and wife accept each other completely and remain open to God's will for their family size.

QUESTIONS TO PONDER

Am I willing to consider Natural Family Planning in our marriage as a means to increase our chances of becoming pregnant or to postpone pregnancy for a serious reason? How do I feel about my answer?

_____

_____

_____

_____

_____

_____

_____

_____

_____

_____

_____

_____

_____

_____

_____

_____

_____

Do I see Natural Family Planning as a way to strengthen and deepen our love for one another? How do I feel about my answer?

_____

_____

_____

_____

_____

_____

_____

_____

_____

_____

_____

_____

_____

_____

_____

_____

_____

_____

_____

Do I see Natural Family Planning as a way for us to cooperate with God in determining our family size? How do I feel about my answer?

_____

_____

_____

_____

_____

_____

_____

_____

_____

_____

_____

_____

_____

_____

_____

_____

AFTERWORD

Jesus Christ made marriage a sacrament with his first miracle at the wedding in Cana. The fact that his first miracle established this sacrament indicates the importance of marriage in God's saving plan. When the Pharisees asked Jesus if divorce was lawful, he replied, *"They are no more two, but one flesh. What therefore God has joined together, don't let man tear apart" (Matthew 19:6).* They persisted and asked why Moses had permitted divorce, and Jesus replied that it was because of the hardness of their hearts, *"but from the beginning it has not been so"* (Matthew 19:8).

Marital love should be permanent or it is not truly love. Love is not a feeling but an act of the will. We cannot depend on our own human strength to overcome whatever temptations enter our married lives, but on the grace of God within us. Building our marriages on the cross of Christ, the ultimate sign of God's love for us, reassures us that we have a well of infinite grace from which we can draw all that we need to persevere.

God has a stake in every marriage, for through each

couple he continues to build a world of love as they exemplify the love he has for his people. In the Sacrament of Matrimony where the marriage is between two Christians, the husband and wife are called to reveal the love that Christ has for his bride, the Church, as St. Paul so beautifully described in Ephesians,

> *For this cause a man will leave his father and*
> *mother and will be joined to his wife.*
> *Then the two will become one flesh.*
> *This mystery is great, but I speak concerning*
> *Christ and the assembly.*

> --Ephesians 5:31-32

The world can catch a glimpse of the love poured out on us through the Cross in the self-sacrificing and unconditional love that husband and wife are called to live. Married couples don't have to settle for a marriage that is just "fine." Instead, they can grow more deeply and passionately in love with each other every day. Then their love can overflow to their children and everyone around them. Husbands and wives can receive abundant graces to carry them through their struggles and lift them higher than they ever could have imagined.

QUESTIONS TO PONDER

Do I believe that God should be at the center of our marriage? How do I feel about my answer?

_____

_____

_____

_____

_____

_____

_____

_____

_____

_____

_____

_____

_____

_____

_____

_____

_____

_____

_____

Do I believe that God will give us the grace to live out our wedding vows? How do I feel about my answer?

_____

_____

_____

_____

_____

_____

_____

_____

_____

_____

_____

_____

_____

_____

_____

_____

_____

_____

Do I believe that love is not a feeling but a decision, an act of the will? How do I feel about my answer?

_____

_____

_____

_____

_____

_____

_____

_____

_____

_____

_____

_____

_____

_____

_____

_____

_____

_____

_____

Do I believe that we are called to greatness in our marriage? How do I feel about my answer?

_____

_____

_____

_____

_____

_____

_____

_____

_____

_____

_____

_____

_____

_____

_____

_____

_____

Do I believe that our marriage will last until death parts us? How do I feel about my answer?

_____

_____

_____

_____

_____

_____

_____

_____

_____

_____

_____

_____

_____

_____

_____

_____

_____

_____

_____

_____

Do I believe that our marriage reflects the love of God for his people? How do I feel about my answer?

_____

_____

_____

_____

_____

_____

_____

_____

_____

_____

_____

_____

_____

_____

_____

_____

_____

_____

_____

Do I believe that as the Sacrament of Matrimony we are called to reveal the love that Jesus Christ has for his Church, the people of God? How do I feel about my answer?

_____

_____

_____

_____

_____

_____

_____

_____

_____

_____

_____

_____

_____

_____

_____

_____

_____

BIBLIOGRAPHY

Word English Bible (Catholic)

Catechism of the Catholic Church (Libreria Editrice Vaticana, 1994)

Book of Common Prayer, The Episcopal Church (1979), Oxford University Press

Pope Paul VI, *Humanae Vitae*

Gary Chapman, *The Five Love Languages* (Chicago: Northfield Publishing, 1992)

Neil Clark Warren, *How to Know if Someone Is Worth Pursuing in Two Dates or Less* (Nashville: Thomas Nelson Publishers, 1999)

Evelyn Waugh, *Brideshead Revisited* (New York, Boston, London: Little, Brown and Company, 1944)

CPSIA information can be obtained
at www.ICGtesting.com
Printed in the USA
LVHW101017030422
715188LV00004B/190